For Winnie

... with hopes that someday you'll find a passion like I did.

ISBN 978-1-08-138594-1

THE NINE VIRTUES OF GOLF

ESSAYS, MUSINGS, AND OTHER CONTEMPLATIONS ON THE GAME

Written by
JAY REVELL

Foreword by
TOM COYNE

CONTENTS

FOREWORD

The only thing better than reading Jay Revel's reflections on golf is playing it with him. I have been fortunate to do so a few times—at his beloved childhood hang of Havana Golf & Country Club and at his home club of Capital City in Tallahassee. He's a very fine player, which isn't always the case with golf writers. But more important than what Jay scores in any given round is how much he takes from it—from each swing and step, and each quiet moment of unexpected significance.

Golf is a great game for writing types—the best game, I'm sure Jay would agree—for the moments it gives us to ponder, pause, and consider our lives. These moments lead to pages, if we do the work of putting it all down onto paper, and Jay has done so for years with discipline and sensitivity and a keen eye for the gifts golf provides us when we are open to receiving them. In this collection, you'll have a chance to not just relive some of Jay's golf epiphanies but to recognize your own within them. We all share the same questions and curiosities; it's the writer's job to set them down somewhere, and let a reader connect with them. And just as it's easy work to connect with Jay as a golf partner, so is it to connect with his words, finding your golfing self in the questions he puts forth and the answers he discovers.

The big question that all writing wrestles with has always been: Why do people do the things they do? Authors attack it from myriad angles and styles, but we all read for some insight into the human condition and some guidance along our life's path. Ever since we were sitting around fires in caves scratching stories onto walls, it has been in our DNA to need stories: to hear how the hunter got the bear, or how the bear got him, so that we might do the same or do better. We're programmed to listen so as to learn, and when the details are ripe and the lessons wise, we feel a connection to those stories in our bones. I think that's the experience you will have here in these pages, where there is much for us to learn and realize and remember about our own walk through life or our walk down a fairway. As Jay makes clear, the two overlap in the most wondrous ways.

— *Tom Coyne*

Introduction

There is nowhere I feel more at home than on a golf course. I grew up on a golf course, my first job was on a golf course, and today my most enjoyable days are spent on the golf course with my family, friends, and dogs. Golf has always been a foundational element in my life, and as I grow older my appreciation for the game has become a fuel for writing about it.

Naturally, as I've come to write more frequently about the game, the pieces that mean the most to me are the ones that reflect the role golf plays in my everyday life. Oddly enough, those are also the stories that generate the most feedback from my readers.

What I've come to discover through writing about golf is that the game is personal to most people who play it. Almost everyone has their own collection of stories about the people and places that shaped their understanding of the game. While I love to write about history, course architecture, interesting characters, and hotly debated topics in the sport, what keeps me coming back to my keyboard is a desire to connect with people who have a deep personal relationship with golf. My avenue for doing that is sharing stories that speak to my experiences in the game and how it has shaped who I am.

As a writer, I love the opportunity to describe the feelings which can only be generated through playing golf. I like to believe that I have some skill in that field, but there is one feeling I still struggle to convey to those who read my work. Somewhere down in my chest, likely between my heart and the bottom of my stomach, there is an uneasiness that

I have yet to overcome. It starts as a knot-like feeling and evolves into something approaching a panic attack. It usually begins each time I have an idea for a story and gets worse as I work up the courage to write it. The best I can do is self-diagnose this feeling as a burning desire to share how golf is connected to my soul.

Writing about golf was not a lifelong dream and it is still not quite a career, but with each passage I put to paper, I find that perhaps this is what I'm meant to do. Like most things in life and golf, writing about the game has been quite the journey. My efforts began a few years ago when I started having that previously described feeling in my chest. I felt compelled to express what golf had done to save my life, so I started typing and I haven't stopped since.

There were years where I was estranged from golf. I swore off the game after a post high school burnout, and through college I treated it more as a thing I used to do. Life brought me back around though. The desire to play crept back in over time. Through some travel, local competitions, and constant reading about golf, I developed a new and lasting infatuation with the game. After my collegiate hiatus, golf came back with a vengeance. Those old familiar feelings returned, and my love for golf was resurrected. This time that passion for golf manifested through my words.

Once golf came to occupy a certain amount of my time again, my mind began to race with ideas for stories that I'd like to write. Unfortunately, other than the professional writing and many graduate school papers on the subject of politics, I had no idea what I was doing. With some raw ability and a notebook full of concepts for stories, I began to sketch out some pieces based on my travels and other items in the game that I found interesting.

Armed with a Twitter account and a Medium page, I set out to find some sort of audience. What has transpired since then still leaves me humbled. Over the past few years, as I've published a variety of stories, essays, and other musings on golf, I've found thousands of people who feel the same way I do about the game.

I remain moved by the idea that anyone will take the time to read my simple golf stories. I believe that one of the most valuable things someone can give you is their time and attention, and I am forever grateful for every reader that has done so for me. The fact that people still click on my links, visit my site, and read what I write fills me with an incredible joy.

Golf feels like a bigger community today than ever before. As much as I enjoy writing about the game, what I've really come to covet is the nearness to others who share my sensibilities for it. The stories that I write are all united by a common desire to connect with other golfers who can't get enough of this silly, agonizing, painstaking, excruciating, embarrassing, joyful, wondrous, exhilarating, life changing, and fulfilling game.

Which brings me to this book. What follows this introduction is a collection of my favorite pieces from my first few years writing about golf. I chose these works because out of what I've written to date, they are the closest reflection of my golfing soul. These essays and other writing devices are presented as a greatest hits album of sorts, and I'm hopeful this is only volume 1.

If there is any common theme among the writings in this book, it is simply that they show the many reasons I have for loving golf and the people who play it. Put me on a golf course with the people I love—true golfers that is—and I'll be right at home. You never know, I might even write a story about it.

1

The Nine Virtues of Golf

The game of golf and its role in the life of those who play it is worthy of regular contemplation. In particular, the virtues associated with the game require constant consideration. The golfer who seeks out these virtues is one who searches for a more properly balanced life.

Golf was created with specific etiquette and rules as a way of designing a game that mirrors life. Those rules and traditions are all modeled from virtues that are commonly believed to be the pillars of a successful existence. There are three sets of virtues that are inherently built into the fabric of golf. These are the Foundation Virtues, the Attitude Virtues, and the Realization Virtues.

The Foundation Virtues

Every structure must begin with the building of a strong foundation. The golfer is no different.

Accountability

Golfers must look inward to find the source of both good swings and bad. Only the player can swing his or her club in this game. The strokes that are tallied on the scorecard are made by the golfer and nobody else. Every golfer must understand this and make ample preparations through practice in order to find success. To be a golfer of any regard, you must learn to be accountable to yourself.

Integrity

There are rules here, and you are asked to enforce them on yourself. No task is more difficult in the chase of victory, and no test is more revealing about one's character. Integrity must be developed through a devotion to higher ideals. The golfer's sense of honesty should be beyond reproach.

Patience

Good things take time. There are no shortcuts in golf, and the game's greatest hazards are disguised to entrap those who seek them. Golf is designed to challenge those who are hurried the most while rewarding the more methodical mindset. Golf requires a steady offering of the one thing we have the least of—golf asks us for our time. Well rewarded is the patient golfer.

The Attitude Virtues

Attitude is everything in golf. The mindset that you bring to a challenge will determine whether or not you can rise to conquer it.

Humility

Humble thyself or the game will do it for you. No other sporting pursuit will bring an impassioned player to their knees like golf. The golfer must know the limits of their game and appreciate the will of the golf gods. Understanding the boundary of one's ability and the fate of uncontrollable outcomes is the key to achieving the best possible score. Always be prepared for the bad bounce and the winds of misfortune as they find us all at some point in the game.

Gratitude

Be gracious at all times, and remember that golf is a game for ladies and gentlemen. It is an honor to be a golfer, and any day on the course is deserving of robust appreciation. The golfer should be thankful for the privilege of playing and conduct oneself in accordance with the knowledge that every round could possibly be their last.

Confidence

As a golfer, you must believe in your abilities in order to score well. To play good golf you must first believe that you can do so. The golfer must stand tall and swing with conviction. Pitches and putts should be struck with authority. Confidence is not an invitation to display bravado nor is it a tool of the braggadocios, but instead a fuel for a golfer's best possible performance.

The Realization Virtues

Golf is a journey. The destination is not found but realized through a deliberate process. Inward reflection leads to outward improvement.

Generosity

To be a golfer is to be a giver. Remember that someone once gave you the gift of golf, and it is your duty to share the game with others. Golf will offer you an endless amount of personal growth, and only you can know how to best give back to the game. The golfer should be charitable with both their time and money as a means for helping others through the game. The rewards of such giving far outweigh any other achievements in golf.

Respect

Be a golfer who subscribes to the golden rule. To earn respect, one must first give respect to others. The game should be respected as well. Hold fast to this fading commodity, and you will benefit while lifting those around you. Begin each round with a respect for the course, your fellow players, and everything that golf stands for, and you will never have a bad experience. This begins by finding and appreciating the value in everything. Do so and others will find the same in you.

Wisdom

The journey of a golfer is a lifelong search for understanding. The game holds many secrets, but they can only be mined through years of careful study. The path to discovering the truths of golf is winding and erratic, but every step along the walk will yield some trace amount of wisdom. Heavy is the bag that is filled with the collection of these lessons from a lifetime in golf. The weight of this wisdom is no burden, but rather the ballast used to steady your vessel. Be ever seeking the wisdom that only golf can grant.

Golf reminds us that life is best enjoyed in accordance with the virtues reflecting the most laudable of human qualities. The well-lived golf life is firmly grounded in a strong foundation, an appreciative attitude, and a firm realization of what makes the game stay so uniquely tethered to our souls. The virtuous golfer will relish the opportunity to play the game knowing that it is a means to achieving the betterment of oneself.

2

How I Got Hooked on Golf

If golf is a drug, then I was raised in an opium den. Havana Golf & Country Club is the social epicenter of the single stoplight town I grew up in. When I was young, I was convinced that this little nine-hole golf club was the center of the universe. Today, I know it was just the center of mine.

Havana Golf & Country Club was founded in the early 1960s as a place for the town's farming citizens and working class to recreate. Routed over an old tobacco farm, the golf course is short, easy to walk, and built for a laid-back lifestyle. My grandfather was the golf professional at the club, and my house was just off the fourth hole. Every day was a golf day for me. My proximity to golf, when paired with our small town's lack of entertainment options for children, was like giving a young pyromaniac a box of matches and a forest to play in.

The addiction took hold early. Somewhere under the hot sun of a childhood summer, my grandfather began to seriously teach me the game. He told me, "I'm going to show you how to hook the ball, and I want you to spend your whole life fighting it." He wrapped my young hands around a cracked old golf grip and helped me find my infatuation.

As I ventured into adolescence, the Havana Golf & Country Club became a beacon that called to me daily. In my youth, I spent every waking moment soaking up the atmosphere of the club. I found myself drawn to the people who loved to play the game there. The men that frequented the club were like living legends to a small boy who dreamed of playing like them someday.

The cast of characters that called our club home was like something from a Faulkner novel. Many of them could have been regular cast members of The Andy Griffith Show. I have vivid memories of their larger-than-life personas. Most of all I remember their passion for playing golf. These men lived to play and played to live. They were at home on the course and spent their time and money surrendering to the whims of the game.

I remember men like Cotton Jackson. He was tall, slender, blue jean-clad with a cigarette on his lip, and had a vicious short game. Every time he saw me, he yelled out, "How 'bout it young lad!" before inquiring about the state of my game. There were some serious sticks in Havana. David Touchton was known as "Mr. Smooth" and was a hell of a player. His left-handed and effortless swing was symphonic in nature. When he made a turn at the ball, it sounded like a candle being blown out. There were a hundred more guys just as interesting and entertaining out there every day.

These were the kind of men who made up the gangsome every Saturday and Sunday afternoon at 1 p.m. Forty some odd players lined up on the putting green on those weekend afternoons chasing a few dollars before the shotgun start. The bets these gentlemen made were small in nature but large in importance. When they let me start playing with them, I felt like I had just earned my tour card.

These men taught me how to cuss, play cards, and grind out pars. More importantly, they taught me how to be a champion for camaraderie and competition on the course. They dumped gasoline on a spark that my grandfather created when he put my hands against a club for the first time.

These passionate players were my heroes growing up. So naturally, I set out to master the game they all loved. Havana gave me the opportunity to dive into the depths of my swing, and I spent days on end hitting shots and chasing my golfing dreams.

My exploration into the golf swing occurred under the shade of a pecan tree that sat at the back of the driving range. Each day I pulled a rickety rust bucket of a range picker behind a golf cart to earn a few bucks. The club let me hit as many balls as I liked as long as I left the field clean picked afterward. I would hit balls well into the dark while wearing down the ground around the pecan tree. When the tree toppled some years later, I assumed that my decimation of the root system was at fault.

When I wasn't on the range, I was at the pro shop. The pro shop is separate from the clubhouse, and it has always served as the primary hang for the members. The building is made of red brick with a living room-style lounge area that is centered around a fireplace. Overlooking that room is a wraparound counter that long served as my grandfather's workstation. There at his post, he checked players in, sold drinks and snacks, and peddled golf gear with advice and tall tales.

On the back of the pro shop door, my grandfather recorded my childhood height by carving a notch with his pocket knife every few months. Those traces of my upbringing are still ascribed in that door jam. There are plaques on the wall with the names of my idols listed for winning club championships, and over on the bookshelf is a trophy named for my grandfather that I managed to get my name etched on once. That's likely the only Hall of Fame I'll ever make it in for my golf conquests, but I'm damn proud of it.

Out on the porch is where the evening drinks were consumed by the regulars. As the sun reached its sinking point on the horizon each night, these men would sit in rocking chairs with relaxing company and a stiff drink to sip. From that shared perch, they all watched me on the putting green a few feet away. I worked on perfecting my putting stroke while they told me stories that encouraged me on my path to becoming a golf junkie.

My grandfather retired just before I started high school, but my service to the club was just beginning. I was hired to run the carts and mow the greens. There is something incredibly therapeutic about dropping mower reels onto the morning dew and sweeping it away with a fresh cut of the grass. To this day, I think it was the best job I ever had. I learned so much about golf courses during those summer days that now shape my beliefs about the game. It's hard to describe the appreciation you develop for a golf course when you are the one mowing it.

My days and nights at Havana Golf & Country Club built a dependency for golf deep inside my soul. I can't imagine my life without the game. My wife will probably never understand what happens to me when I'm deprived of this pastime, but over the years and many trips back to Havana, I think it has started to make sense. My relationship with golf is symbiotic. If you remove it from me, you remove part of me and I'm afraid of what I might seek out to fill that void.

Golf at Havana was my first love. In a small town where there weren't many kids around, it was the golf course that became my best friend. We took long walks together, made memories when no one else was watching, and shared secrets about each other that most folks wouldn't understand. My small-town course never felt inadequate to me. It was always someplace special, and when I go back there, I still feel that way.

Many of the old-timers are gone now, and Havana doesn't have games as big as it once did. The course has lost some great characters, but it hasn't lost its charm. There is a gaggle of golfers that gather on the porch each day, and occasionally there is a youngster learning the game on the same putting green I used to mow. My golfing dreams are buried somewhere under the stump of a pecan tree, but what I learned about the game there will stay with me forever.

My life is uniquely tied to the game of golf. My grandfather made the introduction, and Havana Golf & Country Club served as the backdrop for my discovery of the game. These days I'm fortunate to travel and play at many places across the golfing landscape of America, but there is still no better sight than when I come over the railroad tracks to see the Havana pro shop sitting peacefully on the hill. It's like reliving my favorite first date over and over again.

Small town clubs like Havana once dotted the maps of American golf, and those places raised many a golfing fool like me. As times and tastes have changed, Havana and courses like it have become increasingly rare. Golf is highly addictive, but for the game to take hold in people there must be places where its best qualities and most colorful characters are found in abundance. I was lucky to have a place like that. I know that I'll never be able to shake my addiction, and because of Havana I wear that like a badge of honor.

3

One Last Walk...A Farewell to My Favorite Clubs

A good set of golf clubs can be hard to let go of. Replacing old clubs feels a lot like breaking up, and I've never really been any good at that. I've got a new set of irons that recently arrived in the mail, and once again I have found myself wondering how to bid adieu to a beloved collection of hard-used forged irons.

My old set was with me for a few very fine years. They have a buttery feel that I can sense in my fingertips, and their faces are worn brown in a spot the size of a quarter. They bear the marks and bruises of thousands of miles traveled and many hundreds of holes played. Each of those blemishes represents a swing or a memory from some of the best golfing years of my life, but it's time to turn the page.

I'm quite excited about my new clubs. The steel has an untouched look to it and they almost have that new car smell. They don't know it yet, but they will see the shores of distant lands and soon strike the ground of foreign soil. I needed something new for the next chapter of my travels, and I'm confident in my selection. Yet my old clubs still arouse a feeling of trust and longing when I walk by them in the garage.

I like to keep my old clubs around in case I decide to take them for a spin again. As my wife can attest, I have an ever-growing collection of clubs that occupy almost as much garage space as her Christmas decorations. Every club that I've ever hit a significant shot with still lives in one of my varied golf bags that lean against the wall between a water heater and a shelving unit. My latest addition to that space hasn't quite gotten comfortable there yet. When I walked by them on New Year's Eve, they asked me in a whisper for one last walk.

The afternoon of the last day of the year was fading fast, and I got permission from my wife to go out for a few final swings. I didn't tell her that it was a walk aimed at giving my clubs a proper send-off. She already thinks I'm crazy. No need to confirm it. The clouds of winter had parted, and the sun was flirting with the horizon in a beautiful way. I loaded up my dog Leon and grabbed my clubs to head to the course.

The parking lot was emptying, and the first tee was wide open. My dog led the way, and my clubs got to clang their way down the hill one more time. My game has been as rusty as the faces of my irons, but after finding the first few greens in regulation, I began to get the feel of it again. The old clubs were showing me they still had some magic.

Something was clicking, and it wasn't just the dog tags. My swing was in rhythm, and my clubs were reminding me of all the places we had been together. In each approach, I could recall the swings we made on the Monterey Peninsula and the steps we took around Kiawah Island. I was hearing the call of Colorado again and humming the song of Sweetens Cove. The sunset was lighting up the sky, and I remembered all the ones these clubs and I had seen together.

I knocked it stiff on the fifth and remembered holing out for eagle there the day after my daughter was born. These clubs were with me through life as well as golf. There was the tournament I won with my brother and the nine holes I walked with dad when we found out my grandfather had his stroke. There were some good days and some difficult ones, but we were together for them all.

Before I knew what was happening, I had made three birdies in four holes. My trusted old friends were showing me what they were still capable of. Maybe they thought it was an audition for another year in the bag. Things just came easy that evening. Much like it did for the few seasons before fatherhood that saw me learn how to win again. It was these clubs that made that run happen.

When we walked up the ninth hole, the sun was all but gone. The kids in the neighborhood were starting to light firecrackers, and my beloved dog was getting twitchy. My clubs and I had made some fireworks of our own for our last nine holes. When it was over, I had managed to shoot one under par for the walk. It was a score that was not only unanticipated but one I likely would have forgotten to keep had I not snapped out of my trance.

These clubs had put a spell on me again. They let me swing them once more in the way that I once knew how. I hit all but one green and smiled from start to finish. Had the sun not disappeared into a new year, we would have probably stayed out all night. Unfortunately, we were done with the round and done with our time together.

I gave the clubs a good wipe down before we headed home, and Leon kept them company in the back of the car. When we got to the house, I opened the garage and there in the corner my old clubs found their new home. The next time I walk they won't be with me, but I'll always have them close by just in case.

I've had a few fun nights on New Year's Eve in my life, but I think the nine holes I played with those old sticks was my best. December 31 isn't an ideal date for a breakup, but then again, I've never really been good at that. You never know when I might need to bring them out for a few more swings.

4

Scotland Down the Street

Somewhere in another lifetime, I'd live in Scotland. I'd live in a small city by the sea where a unique links course is the center of the community. I'd go for walks by morning light with a coffee and a putter in my hands. Evenings would be spent repeating the same links routine with my clubs in tow and a dog by my side. In that life I would play every day, and the pub owners down the street would all know me by my first name.

In reality, I don't have another lifetime to live. I likely won't ever live the life of a golfer in a city by the sea. What I do have is a wonderful wife, a beautiful baby, and a great job. I have a happy home, a convenient golf course, and a love for the life God gave me. Some days I dream of living that Scottish golf life, but in reality, I have to find that Scotland dream in the life I love at home.

Our city isn't by the sea, and my course isn't a links. However, I have found that with a little suspension of disbelief, my neighborhood can be my Scotland. I can live my dream golf life if I am willing to step out of the American norms of how the game works.

My house sits just a few blocks from the golf course. Between me and the greens are my neighbors, our parks, and a short walk down the street. After many years of dreaming about the Scottish style of life, I decided to make it for myself right here at home.

I swore off the golf cart and downsized my bag. I put my car keys down and grabbed the dog leash. I took out my modern metals and put in a set of persimmons. I let go of what I had been told was golf, and I created a world where the game is purer and the experience is more memorable.

My walk to the golf course has become a highlight of my days. Sometimes it is on a Sunday morning with my pup and a 4 wood. On the way to the course, we can smell the bacon cooking from an open window of the house by the park. I sip coffee and stroll with a pocket full of pellets on the way to hit some shots before the morning groups make the back nine.

Other evenings I'll have a leash in hand and my lightweight bag over my shoulder. I stop and talk to my neighbor planting a tree in his yard, and the people passing in cars look at me funny. A man, a dog, a golf bag, and some tartan head-covers stand out on the busy street corner. It looks different because it is different.

I quit keeping scores, but I do keep a dog treat on hand. I try shots I normally would forgo, and I even find the fun in failing. I walk a few holes and maybe play some backward. I chase for a moment a scene that I saw somewhere in my mind. My golf world seems upside down to some, but by God, it feels right to me.

The dog gets unleashed when we cross from the street to the fairways. We both find a little bit of freedom out there. He from the restraint I put on him and me from the restraints I've long accepted from the game. We can't smell the sea, but we can pretend for a few hours a week that the world we live in and the world we dream of is indeed the same place.

The walk home has its moments, too. The kids playing in the park ask me why I'm carrying my clubs, and my response comes with a smile. I tell them that I'm a golfer and that I love to walk and play. They don't understand now but somewhere in a distant daydream, they will seek a place of refuge from the restrictions of the life they live. They may not dream of Scotland, but I hope they can someday summon their childlike imagination to take them somewhere they seek to be.

Some nights I pass by joggers when my pup and I head home. I can't help but wonder what they must think. How strange it must be for those people who believe they are in their neighborhood, while I know it's really Scotland.

When we get to the garage and hang up the clubs and leash, my dog and I are back from a distant land. Scotland may be far from home, but when we walk and play it's not too far from our reach. I've got a wife I want to kiss and a baby I love to hug. There are bills to pay and a yard to mow. I'll need to be in the office early the next day, too. Life is real, and Scotland is thousands of miles away, but when I walk my dog to the course now, I can hear the waves lapping on the shore and the bagpipes playing in my head.

Golf in Scotland is a pastime and a way of life. Golf in America is, well, something different. I dream of living a golf life in the land where the game began. It's a dream that I have found a way to live on the walk from home to the course. The only thing I need now is a pub down the street—preferably one that doesn't mind golf clubs and dogs.

5

Golf in My Favorite Gangsome

"Well boys, I managed to get away for a few hours. Glad to be with you again. Hopefully, Tom won't stick me in damn a fivesome. I need to get home at a decent hour."

That's a variation of the regular lines I deliver to my friends upon arrival at my golf club. I utter these words or something similar while my group warms up for another round together. The routine rarely varies. The range is always packed as we prepare for our regular game on the old home course. I walk up just in time to hear our teams for the day.

"Ok guys, we've got fifteen players. Three teams today."

I shake my head as Tom shouts out the names of the teams. We gather round to listen for our playing partners and snicker when we are dealt a bad hand. Tom has the unfortunate duty of arranging the squads each weekend, but for some reason he loves it. I guess everyone needs a shtick even if it's the only job more thankless than being the club president. Each week the gang gathers near the first tee in anticipation of knowing who they'll blame the loss of twenty dollars later that afternoon. All eyes on Tom.

The group plays at 10:30 a.m. each Saturday and Sunday. The dew sweeping super-seniors go off early, but the middle of the day is reserved for us. We like to occupy the course during the hours set aside for guys whose wives detest their golfing habits the most. When you play from 10:30 a.m. to 2:30 p.m., you wipe away the hopes your wife had for any kind of spousal productivity that day.

I'm in the camp that can't get away with two days of golf in a weekend anymore, but many of these guys still pull it off somehow. These days I'm more of a once a month participant in our habitual outing. This is good for my marriage but my frequent absences further reduce the weight of my arguments against Tom's proclivity for fivesomes.

Many of my weekends get filled with the honey-do lists and other matters of husbandry, but sometimes I still hit the marital lottery. When I get a free pass to play with the guys, I try to make the most of it.

I'm a want-to-be golf purist, but I still like to wallow in the spoils of a Saturday at the country club. I'll argue against five players in a group and I always walk, but I still like a few frothy beers, some first tee smack talk, and a generous gimmie or two on the greens. This gangsome offers those attributes in spades.

We indulge in a bit of gentle gambling as well. Our game is a $20 buy-in, and there are four bets in play. We have the best one ball from the team on the front and back nine, the best two balls from the team on all eighteen, and a simple skins game as well. These bets are just big enough to trigger some emotion on the course, but most outbursts are incited by pride. Chest thumping is the real tender of exchange among friends.

Throughout the hours of our battle, the screams of both frustration and achievement echo across our fields of play.

"Yaaaaddddiiiii..."

"Son of a bitch!"

"Booooom!"

The sounds of joy and sorrow are born from moments like an unexpected putt being holed or perhaps a hurried chip being flubbed. These most human of reactions create shrieking hymns that ring through the hills of our club like the bells of Rome.

When we march around the grounds of the club, it's easy to sense how the teams are playing. There are always signs to indicate the mood. If things are progressing as planned, there will be the talk of strategy and chuckles of amusement between fist bumps and high fives. However, when the scoring gets sideways, it's more like being on the Bataan Death March with men whose mounting disappointment is only offered a reprieve from an oncoming cart girl. If you play with us long enough, you'll get plenty of time to sample this full range of impassioned reactions on display.

Every time I make it out to play, it's like seeing another installment of my favorite sitcom. Each game is a singular episode in a long-running syndication that features the various mixtures of our golfing personas. Some guys pair well and others don't, but no matter the arrangement, there is sidesplitting comedy produced from this four-hour affair. Pick any name from our regular roster, and you'll find a reliable source for a post-round story.

Once we finish playing, the settling of our wagers makes for a separate and equally unique variety of theatre. The action occurs on a table of draft beer and chicken wings. On this stage, we hash out who owes what over a chorus of heckling voices.

"I told you that back nine was a winner!"

"Thank god you made that putt on four!"

"Y'all shot what!?"

Drama builds when each troupe arrives in the grill to discover the fate of their fortunes. Some teammates are all smiles while preparing to soak themselves in raining cash. Others who were dealt a losing hand by Tom's team-making sulk into the sofa while clinging to some fading hope that the elusive birdie they made will hold up for a skin.

A sad voice from the back of the room utters, "Anybody birdie eight?"

No one is getting rich from our game, but the braggadocios nature of the scorecard roundup can make us feel like kings if only for half an hour. The room fills up for a feast of fools and the mixture of laughter and bullshit makes for a soundtrack that only good friends can produce. The topics of conversation may differ but the voices around the table don't change much. These are the rituals that keep us coming back.

After the bets are paid and small bills are exchanged, I start looking at my watch while checking for "time to come home" texts from my wife. Our beloved bartender knows the batting order for who has to leave first. He can write up your ticket based on where the clock hands are positioned. He looks at his timepiece and then back at me signaling that I've hit my limit.

I polish off the last drops of golden draft beer and start patting my pockets in search of my wallet. The chicken wings have been reduced to a platter of bone, and the conversation around me turns to who is playing tomorrow. I may be leaving, but the meeting can't be adjourned until the next day's roster is shaped. This is when Marcus starts his call for an emergency nine holes.

"Hey boy, you stick around for the birdie game. Just a quick nine holes. Maybe eleven."

I'm rising from my chair and collecting my items, but he persists.

"Tell her you'll be home soon. Just a birdie game—$2 per pop. You got this. Let's hit it."

The vagaries of the grill room make for predictable conclusions to each week's follies, but regardless of the happenings of the day, the final outcomes remain the same. Usually, I linger a bit too long and scratch my head as I fork over the rest of my cash. On the way out of the door,

I tell the boys "I'll hope to see you next month" before I make a final remark to Tom about the teams he made that day. Meanwhile, the die-hards who have long since achieved endless golf freedoms through sheer will or divorce buckle in their bags for one more turn around the course.

When I walk towards the parking lot, I hear Marcus shout to me, "Ain't too late to join boy! You better get home and be good for your girls though!"

He knows I'd love to put my spikes back on, but my time is typically up. I climb into my car and when I pull away, I see draft beer spilling from a cup holder as his cart bounces down the path to playing more golf. Some things never change.

I take comfort in knowing that when I'm granted permission from home, I can find and participate in this golfing circus on any given weekend. This gangsome plays across every season. Birthdays, holidays, anniversaries, or weather all be damned, there is always a group on the tee at 10:30 waiting for a playing assignment from Tom. The unmatched hilarity of it all makes for my favorite manner of amusement. Hopefully, I can make it out to play in the group again soon.

6

Carry Your Clubs

Carry your clubs and hear them clang
as one foot follows the other.
Walk the course with your eyes up
searching for scenes to discover.

Feel the weight of the bag you tote
filled with hope on your shoulder.
Leave the cart behind when you play
knowing that you can be bolder.

Enjoy the time required
to tarry between each shot.
Look out and take the course in
while you make a steady trot.

Admire the grass, wind, water, and earth
as you stroll with sky above.
Carry your clubs, walk, and remember
why golf is the game you love.

7

Golf on Common Ground

There is no bond quite like that which exists between brothers. It is also true that there are few arguments as intense as those that involve siblings. Oftentimes those disagreements can last for years if not decades, and I've always been afraid of that happening in my family.

My brother and I could probably pass for strangers. Our parents insist that we are of the same blood, but upon first glance, most folks might need some convincing. Sometimes I do too. We don't look alike, act alike, or think alike, but we do have one great commonality...we both love golf.

Hilton and I live and often feel far apart from each other, but golf remains our shared language. Even still, I'm certain that we speak different dialects. However distant our worldviews and idiosyncrasies may be, we have found some ability to bridge our divide when golf serves as our translator.

Hilton and I tend to be the yin to each other's yang, and that is especially evident on the golf course. The game brings us together in a way that we both need. Despite our differences, golf allows us to be close with each other, even if it's only in four-hour increments.

When my brother and I play golf, we are separated from the worldly matters that drive our holiday conversations into debates. Golf provides us the chance to be together in deliberate isolation and find our common ground again. Although our differences are as stark as day and night, golf tends to blur the lines a bit.

Hilton has long dark hair, and he wears it regularly in a ponytail or man-bun. He prefers hiking sandals to shoes and enjoys living in the lax Colorado legal environment with his longtime girlfriend. He's about my height but skinny and a naturally gifted athlete and musician. His politics are left of Bernie Sanders, and he regularly speaks about offbeat political matters and conspiracy theories. He is nearly my polar opposite in every way.

I work for a business interest group in Florida and have a bit of what I call "office weight." I'm a married man with an infant daughter, and I can't get enough of my family. I've got a mortgage and a country club membership to match my master's degree and generally conservative disposition. My brother often looks at me like I'm an asshole, and sometimes I'm afraid he might be right.

We act as most brothers do. Competing for parental affection and approval is a constant. We still like to bicker and fight over trivial things as we did in the back of mom's Ford Explorer on the way to junior golf tournaments. I know I'm right, and so does he. We are four years apart in age, and from what I can gather that's just the right amount of time for the habits and traits of one brother to not rub off on the other. We don't have much in common besides our ancestry, but thankfully we grew up on a golf course, and the gravitational pull of that childhood love still brings us together on occasion.

Golf is a release for each of us in very different ways. Hilton sees golf as pure fun. He checks out from work; forgets about the ring he'll need to buy someday and looks to catch a buzz while chasing birdies. Meanwhile, I see golf as a meditation. I find peace in the solitude of the game, hear poetry in the sound of a swing, and believe that golf is uniquely tethered to my soul. Hilton equates golf to a Grateful Dead concert, and I treat it more like a day on Walden Pond. When we play, it is the equivalent of a disk jockey teeing it up with a transcendentalist.

Hilton normally plays where he can find a good deal. He hates golf shoes and tucked in shirts and plays barefoot when allowed. He enjoys nice courses and loves the game but couldn't care less about my passion for its history and architecture. Based on his attire, he could probably be a good stand-in at any municipal course in America, but one look at his game would give away his pedigree.

Our grandfather taught us how to play when we were kids. Gramps was the head pro at our small-town club, and he nurtured our games all the way through high school. Our uncle played on tour, and we spent many summers watching him on the road. Golf was an everyday obsession in our family. Most nights after dinner were spent in chipping contests with Dad, and many days we played until dark while walking our dog. Golf runs deep in all of us, and it remains the strength of my relationship with Hilton.

When Hilton and I play together, it is as if the golf gods are overseeing peace talks between regularly warring nations. The golf course is sacred ground, and no battles are to be fought there. When we cross the threshold from the parking lot to the grass, we enter a sort of demilitarized zone. Golf becomes a buffer between us and the bullshit that we have a hard time letting go of in other settings.

There were many years in which we didn't play so much. We both became lost in the journey to who we are as adults, and our days on the golf course together were seldom. It was in those times in which the differences we had developed on the way to adulthood became a breeding ground for animosity. Playing golf together became a relic of our childhood, and I was worried about whether or not we'd ever reconnect. Fortunately for both of us, the maturity of increasing age has resurrected our feelings for both golf and each other.

Golf makes us more capable of being civil. We will always have tense moments, but an invitation to play with each other is an olive branch that we both can recognize. That revelation has opened the door to a whole new chapter in our lives.

In my office, I keep a vast assortment of golf memorabilia, trophies, and other objects that denote my adventures in the game. Among those treasures, my most prized possessions are from memories made while playing with Hilton. I have our small-town newspaper framed above my desk which features a headline about how the Revell brothers once won the biggest two-man tournament in town. In addition to that glorious achievement, I have a photo on my bookshelf of the two of us standing on a dune ridge in the vast reaches of the Colorado chop hills at Ballyneal Golf & Hunt Club.

The newspaper clipping makes me smile because it was the first and only time I won that tournament. Even more importantly, it reminds me that in order to win, I had to partner with my oldest and best friend. That was the weekend where Hilton and I found out how to best overcome the barriers between us. Amazingly, it resulted in a series of moments that I'll never forget.

The photo on the shelf is another story entirely. Until we ventured to Ballyneal, the two of us had never traveled together on our own. We steered our way to a place that is as remote as you can imagine in America, and the golf we found there washed away the layers of life that have made us seem so different.

Days like those enshrined on my wall are why I get excited to know when Hilton is coming home next. They are also the reason I stay up late and plot the potential places that we can visit for golf in the years ahead. The game will always be a part of who we are, and it still binds us to our better angels. We have many more holes to play together in this life, and there is still some room in my office for a few more memories to hang.

It is hard to pinpoint where my brother and I chose our different paths in life, but both of them lead back to a small-town country club and a home with our loving parents. I remember when our folks built that house for our growing family to live in. Hilton was just my baby brother, and the golf course was just home. We likely would still be different no matter where we had laid our heads, but because of the game we learned there, we will always know how to find each other. Golf is at the root of our souls, and because of that we really aren't so different after all.

8

The Zen of Backyard Golf

I am standing on the tee box of my new favorite golf hole. There is a club in my hand and hope in my heart. The crispness of the air wraps around me like a calming blanket as I watch the ball sail through the evening light. I observe the orb fall victim to gravity as it lands so close to the pin that my heart pauses to consider the possibilities.

There is glory at this moment, and I am one with the game that I love. My connection to another plane of existence is only broken by the sound of a baby crying through the screen door behind me. Mentally, I am at a links course on the coast of the Scottish Highlands, but in reality, my feet are planted firmly in my backyard.

Suddenly the cliffs of the north coast turn back into boxwood hedges, and I notice my wife is looking at me through the window. I can smell the pasta sauce wafting from the kitchen and hear my one-year-old daughter break into a series of baby sounds. I wiggle my toes to make sure this is real, and I look back at the red flag waving in the gentle breeze some twenty paces away. For ten minutes each night, I come to this place to get lost in my golfing mind. Standing in my yard, I search for some sliver of inner peace while sorting through the list of things I still have to do before the sun goes down.

A few swings of a golf club each day are good for my mental health. Golf is much more than recreation or leisure for me; it's a form of meditation and a release of stress. I don't need eighteen holes to find some stable ground in my mind, but I am a better man when I get some dosage of golf into my system. There is something euphoric about the moment when the club meets the ball, and the chemicals released in my brain bring me to a place of balance and tranquility. Being a father, husband, and full-time executive is not conducive to finding time for golf course therapy, but those duties make me need it more than ever. That's why I built a golf hole in our backyard.

At a certain age, life just starts to accelerate. Family happens, the office consumes you, and at some point, every part of your life feels like work. That is especially true for golf as now I have to make a serious effort just to play. I don't have the luxury of playing whenever I want anymore; instead, I have to negotiate that time against all my other responsibilities. That means that golf gets put on the back burner, but because of my dependency, I have had to make other arrangements. A backyard golf hole allows me to find the mindfulness that only the ancient game can create for me.

I've always been a bit of a schemer, and one night while scooping up some dog poop in the yard, I devised a plan to bring golf closer to home. I drew my inspiration from some of my favorite accounts on social media that showcase unique golf holes only a few steps away from where folks live. Backyard golf holes are not a new phenomenon, but it seems as if the idea is having a renaissance in the age of Instagram. Like many who have come before me, I found myself drawing up ideas for a golf hole just off our back patio.

I had to have a golf hole that I could utilize during the moments in between changing diapers and doing dishes. Space is limited in the backyard, but after a few walks around with a beer in hand I was able to conjure up an ideal layout. It had to be more than just grass though, so I called up the superintendent at our golf club to gain some needed supplies. After explaining my plight to him, he gave me some proper tools to help create my architectural debut. I found some old tee markers and a flag in the cart barn and proceeded to put things in motion.

The hole I designed for myself is a short pitch shot playing downhill from east to west. I built the tee box in a patch of grass between a pathway of brick pavers and the dusty trail my dogs have created. The green site is pitched from left to right between a large pine tree and a small garden bed. The hole is framed by boxwoods and azaleas, and if you squint a little at sundown, you'll swear that it resembles Augusta National. To create some added character, I put up a cast iron bell that is to be rung only in the case of a hole in one.

The variety of grass is not ideal, but it suffices for a playing surface at my low budget course. It actually has responded quite well considering that it receives natural fertilizers from the dogs, and I cut it at the lowest setting possible with my Honda push lawnmower. There is nothing fancy here, but I have found that when I need some minutes to myself and time at the golf course isn't in play, I can retreat to the yard for just enough swings to keep my mind sharp. It is in those brief interludes away from my daily stresses that I remember all that I am grateful for.

What I have created is a place where I can improvise my moments of zen. Maybe it's some form of escapism, but whatever you want to call it, I have found it to be therapeutic. One small pitch shot for golf, one giant leap for Jay's mind.

I visit my short hole at odd hours. Some mornings I wake up early, pour a tall cup of black coffee, and venture out into the yard in my black robe and well-worn slippers for some peaceful swings before the baby wakes up. Other days I show up at home on my lunch break and hit

47

pitch shots before having to return to the office. There are other times as well, like after my wife and I have a debate in the kitchen or I just need to listen to some music and make swings to calm my nerves. In every instance I find myself standing on the tee box of lawn turf focused on the hole and making a small turn to advance the ball toward the target. The simple rhythms of this are soothing to my soul.

A little bit of golf can go a long way toward finding happiness in life, business, and relationships. For me to be effective in any of those realms, I have to be able to be in a good place mentally. Golf gets me there. Despite not being able to run out to the course and play on a whim, I have found a convenient way to create a golf outlet in my very own yard.

My neighbors must wonder about me when they see me standing in my yard holding the finish on a pitch shot. They know I'm up to something related to golf because they see a flagstick waving and balls scattered across the lawn. I doubt they realize its just my version of yoga.

When I wrap my fingers around the grip of my old rusty wedge, I can tune out my troubles and transport to places far away. Some days I'm walking the fairways of Augusta, and on other occasions I'm standing on the cliffs of Scotland's north coast. Maybe I'm listening to the birds chirp through Georgia pines, or perhaps I'm smelling the salty air and gorse blooms near Dornoch. Either way, I'm at ease with the world around me and I can still make it back to help give the baby a bath.

Golf can be anywhere you want it to be. The benefits of the game, in particular, the mental side of it, are not reserved for eighteen holes on a Saturday morning. Instead, golf can be unpacked quite easily just about anywhere you need it.

There are so many variations of the game, and as my time for playing it increasingly disappears, I have found new joy in chasing golf just outside our bedroom window. I think my wife likes this version of the game much better as I'm always within earshot, and I've found a whole new motivation for keeping the grass cut. When she hears the bell ring, she knows I've made another ace and perhaps that I've found some peaceful moment before dinner. Thanks to a backyard golf hole, I've got everything I love all within the confines of home.

9

Daylight Savings Swings

Through yonder fields I walk at dusk
not knowing what I'll find
as I search my soul with swings
and try to leave the day behind.

I play on into the evening
in a constant pursuit of clarity
arriving at that state of mind
with ever-increasing rarity.

I golf my way through summer nights
that I pray will never end
because it's there upon those grassy fields
where my spirit comes to mend.

10

Golf in the Age of Fatherhood

I'll always remember 2018 as the year I became a father. It was also a year I learned a whole new appreciation for golf. My daughter Winnie was born that January, and she changed everything in my life for the better — even golf. When fatherhood found me, I discovered a whole new way of looking at the world. Becoming a dad has not only made me a better man, but it's made me a better golf patron.

Being a dad is incredible, yet the duties of fatherhood tend to make long days on the golf course an increasingly rare occurrence. For those fathers of young children who are golf-obsessed like I am, you'll know what I mean. Having kids creates endless hours of enjoyment but also many hurdles to playing golf regularly.

Every golfing dad finds that the coexistence of a passion for the game and a love for one's family can be frustrating at times. Hours of free time become scarce, being on the course for long stretches makes you feel guilty, and despite your desire to be out playing with friends most times you just can't. As a golfing parent, the lack of playing time can make you cranky, cause you to cancel the country club membership, or even lead you to sell your clubs on eBay for diaper money. It's tough to get out and play as a dad, but I'm here to tell you that this shift in perspective can actually work out to the betterment of your golfing soul.

When I found out that my wife and I were going to have a child, I was in the middle of the best competitive golf season of my adult life. My handicap got down to scratch for the first time since high school, and I won five tournaments that year. I knew it was my last chance to perform at such a level until after my unborn kids get out of college, so I gave it all I had and it paid off. After the ultrasounds started piling up and the nursery got painted, I knew it was time to adopt a new strategy for how I would enjoy the game in the years ahead.

When my daughter was born, I took to reading and writing about the game as much as possible. I found a great deal of inspiration and made it my new mission to discover the spirit of the game rather than constantly testing my skills in it. Through that process of self-discovery, I have found a winning formula for fathers who golf.

My first year as a father yielded five revelations for finding more joy in the game of golf. They are as follows:

1. Play less tournament golf

I love competing in golf, but when Winnie arrived it closed the window on me spending hours practicing for tournaments. I was playing in at least ten to fifteen, two-day golf tournaments each season; since she was born, I've cut that to about three to five events at most. Tournaments are expensive, time-consuming, and unless you are playing well can be a real grind. I gave up almost all tournaments except a few at my home club, and to be honest I'm happier as a golfer. I'd rather spend time and money on a unique golf experience than sweating over four-foot putts with a pro shop gift certificate on the line.

2. Forget about the score

Once I put most tournament golf behind me, I began to realize that my score was much less important than I had always made it out to be. Golf isn't really about what score you make. The game is much more about where you are playing and who you are with. Once I was able to let go of the scorecard, I was open to enjoying varying ways of playing golf. Most times when I play these days, I only use seven clubs in my bag. Not only is the bag lighter on my shoulder, but I have less thinking to do and I play faster. I even started playing with vintage clubs, including persimmon drivers and some hickory irons. I stopped playing for score and started playing for fun again, and that has made a huge difference for me enjoying the game as a golfing dad.

3. Make every trip a golf trip

I'm fortunate to be able to travel from time to time for golf trips, but those are also growing rarer. Since becoming a father, I've looked for creative ways to make every trip I take one that involves golf. When golf time at home decreases, you have to find ways to play on the road. Whether I'm traveling for business, to see family and friends, or even just to get away, I always bring my clubs. Every city has something unique to offer a golfer, and I always plan carefully so that I can get a few holes in while away from home. Some basic internet research will usually reveal that no matter where you are, there is an interesting golf course worthy of experiencing. Even the act of seeking them out is part of the fun.

4. Find the course within your course

When the time for golf gets cut by time for the family, it can become difficult to play even nine holes much less eighteen. Fortunately, at my home course, the routing is such that I can play a wide array of loops that allow me to play in even the shortest of timeframes. My course has loops of 2, 3, 5, 7, 9, 11, and 16 holes all available to me and ending up near the clubhouse. Many courses, particularly those built before 1950, have similar routing features. It is a blast to go out and play two holes on my lunch break or to walk five holes early on a Saturday morning before meeting the girls for breakfast at the club. I have even found ways to play cross-country through one corner of our course and creating new holes entirely. It takes a little imagination to find some routing options that can be played in less than an hour, but sharpening those creative tools will save you time and put you on the course more often.

5. Walk the dog

Multitasking is a great skill set for dads. I've learned to make the absolute best use of my time so that I can still enjoy the many facets of my golf infatuation. I listen to golf podcasts while washing baby bottles, I work on my putting while watching Winnie play on the floor, and most importantly I play golf while I walk the dog. I'm lucky to have a wonderful club that allows me to take my labradoodle Leon with me when I go out to play. I was unsure about trying this at first, but once I saw that Leon was great at tagging along I became hooked on having him with me. Playing golf with a dog is one of the great joys a golfer can experience. Dogs are man's best friend, and I have discovered they are also the perfect playing partner. Take the pup with you and consider yourself marking off an item from your ever-growing list of dad chores.

Being a golf dad isn't easy, but if you are willing to suspend the habits that you have previously ingrained in your golf lifestyle, you can find an even better appreciation for the game while still being a great dad. I encourage you to treat your shrinking windows for golf as an opportunity to explore the variety of the game. My methods may not be perfect for everyone, but if you are a busy dad looking to get back on the course, these tips can serve as a great starting point for building your own model. There is no easy way to quit a full-blown golf addiction cold turkey, so you will need to open your mind to trying something new as a means for getting on the course.

Becoming a father is the best thing to ever happen to me. It just so happens that being a dad has also made me love golf more than ever before. The next challenge will be teaching Winnie how to putt.

11

A Strategic Plan for American Golf:
How to reposition the game for the next generation of Americans

G olf is, at its best, a game for the every-man. Unfortunately, the American version of golf is often the opposite. Somewhere in the last century, our nation's golf industry decided it could "improve" upon the ancient traditions of the game by prioritizing things like exclusivity, lackluster courses, and golf carts. Those policies may have resulted in a temporary boom for the golf industry, but it was unsustainable, and today there are more courses closing in America than opening.

Golf in America is not dead though. The game has found new life in a generation of players who are finding joy through the sport in a variety of non-traditional ways. Golf has a growing presence on social media, short courses and Topgolf are all the rage, and municipal facilities are suddenly cooler than country clubs. We live in a time when American golf is changing for the better, and there is an opportunity at hand to increase the game's popularity. Millennials are now the majority of the workforce, and Gen Z is quickly coming of age, offering golf a window to show both generations that the game can be appealing to them. In order for golf to capitalize on these changing demographics, there needs to be a plan for how to move the game forward in ways that are attractive to these generations.

I believe that can be accomplished by making the future of golf in America resemble the best attributes of the game in Scotland. In Scotland, golf is a resilient game because it is a community pastime. In America, the game was turned into a commodity, strapped on to a cart, and placed behind fences as the result of misguided policies that have been detrimental to the sport. The resulting state of the game is something that is too expensive, unnecessarily slow, and needlessly detached from everyday life. It's time to reexamine how golf in America is offered to the masses. I have great hope that the courses, clubs, companies, and organizations involved in golf can create a bright and thriving future, and it starts by making the game more oriented to the common man.

There are numerous solutions to turning the tide for American golf, but I'd like to offer up a few that I think should be moved to the front of the list. In my belief, the key to creating a new surge in American golfers is to build a nationwide network of courses, facilities, and clubs that are inviting places for passing time with friends and family. American golf should be affordable, walkable, and flexible. We must endeavor to make golf a game that people will choose to play. Golf should be a part of people's lives, not some expensive escape from it. Let's look to create a better golf culture in America and position the game to be a community pastime.

In order to achieve this lofty goal, American golf needs a strategic plan in place to shape how the next two decades should unfold. To begin, the stakeholders of the game need to understand the strengths, weaknesses, opportunities, and threats facing the game today.

Strengths

◊   America has an immense amount of golf courses and millions of players.

◊ Golf is a unique way to discover the variety of American landscapes.

◊ There are more outlets for discovering good golf than ever before.

◊ Current new course construction is generally in good taste.

Weaknesses

◊ American golf is too dependent on golf carts.

◊ The vast majority of courses lack interesting design.

◊ Golf courses have become removed from everyday life.

◊ Too many clubs and courses hold a rigid interpretation of what golf is.

Opportunities

◊ Golf has many attributes that can appeal to millennials (exercise, travel, unique experiences).

◊ There are thousands of golf courses that could become great community assets with some creative design changes.

◊ Golf can be offered in small doses all across the country (short courses, putting courses, Topgolf).

◊ Golf has a fabulous and ever-flourishing relationship with social media.

Threats

◊ Golf takes too long to enjoy for many patrons of the game.

◊ Exclusivity is not an appealing attribute to millennials.

◊ Failed developments, struggling clubs, and a rightsizing of the game have resulted in a sense that "golf is dying."

◊ The cost to enjoy interesting golf is generally too high.

Understanding these factors and their potential impacts on the realities of the sport is critical to completing a successful handoff of golf to new generations. American golf is at a crossroads; in order to create a thriving future, there must be clear and identifiable target outcomes that drive decision-making among stakeholders. Golf's critical stakeholder groups must create a set of imperative priorities to serve as a guiding light in the coming years.

Imperative Priorities

America's golf stakeholders need a universally accepted set of Imperative Priorities that are widely regarded as the compass for which we all use to steer the game. Based on the strengths, weaknesses, opportunities, and threats outlined above, I offer the following four suggestions:

◊   Create open and inviting environments for golf.
◊   Frame golf as a pastime instead of a privilege.
◊   Change the look of golf to better reflect millennial and Gen Z preferences.
◊   Invest in places that promote fun, walkable, and flexible varieties of golf.

Strategic Initiatives

To achieve these desired outcomes, there needs to be a set of initiatives that can appeal to golf's strengths and opportunities while correcting weaknesses and neutralizing threats. American golf needs a combination of both simple policy level changes and more intensive overhauls that require large scale investments. When making a change of this magnitude, small victories are critical to building momentum for larger systematic shifts. The sum of those actions can lead to improved perceptions and newly activated markets for golf. In that spirit, I submit eight strategic initiatives for golf:

Walking must become the preferred way to play the game

As Shivas Irons said, "The game was meant for walking," and it is high time that American golfers got back to this mindset. One of the most important attributes of golf is the time spent walking between shots. It is in those moments where a player can find the unique peace of mind that only a walk on the golf course can offer. When you walk a golf course, you can hear the sounds of nature, see the contours of the land, and better enjoy the company of your companions. The golf cart has ruled the courses of America for far too long. A golf cart is necessary for some who otherwise couldn't play, but most American golfers wrongly see the cart as a must-have accessory. Golf carts make for long rounds and constantly do damage to the course. Meanwhile, walking is great for your health, highly enjoyable, and actually can help you focus and play better. America needs to ditch the cart and encourage the carrying of clubs. To promote walking is to promote the best version of golf.

Private clubs should allow more access

Private golf clubs play an important role in the game. Clubs often serve as the guardians for the traditions and history of golf. Many clubs are also regular hosts to championships and other important tournaments in the sport. The difference between the great clubs of Scotland and the most prestigious clubs in America is how they view public access. In Scotland, clubs see sharing their courses with the public as part of their duty to the game and healthy for the bottom line. Many clubs open their doors a few days a week as a means of sharing the charms of their club and driving outside revenue. Imagine the possibilities if the most important clubs in America adopted such policies. More golfers would travel, fond memories would be created on special occasions, and players could reasonably aspire to someday play the great works of golf design. Now is the time for American clubs to open the gates and share the joys of golf. Golf cannot flourish with its best grounds locked behind gates and hidden from the masses.

Municipal golf must become more interesting

In the next twenty years, the greatest opportunity for golf course architects will be the reimagining of municipal golf. Let's face the facts: There just aren't many new courses being built these days, and that trend has no end in sight. Course architects must partner with municipal governments as a means for rethinking how golf is offered as a service to taxpayers. There is a growing list of projects across the country today that provide a blueprint worth following. Municipal golf should be interesting and diverse. There needs to be more short courses and nine-hole offerings in urban areas where land is limited. The biggest opportunity is renovating existing courses that either under-perform or simply don't deliver a compelling layout. The future of municipal golf is directly tied to the prospects of the broader game. Architects need work, the game needs new players, and citizens need great options for recreation. If we can reposition how governments offer the game, then we can reach millions of potential players. Municipal courses can become the breeding ground for golf's next generation and a godsend for architects.

Match play should be actively promoted

Golf is best played in a match against friends. Match play offers an ideal structure for enjoying competition over a golf course. The scorecard and pencil crowd will find this blasphemous, but golf is more of a sport when played head-to-head in a thrilling match. Match play also lends itself to a variety of formats that are best enjoyed when players are prioritizing the winning of holes versus the final score. Match play makes any course immediately more interesting and allows for a speedy pace of play. The great match play golfers are a dying breed, and that is a real shame. Match play calls for daring shots and bold decision-making at times, while also rewarding the strategic and patient golfer in other moments. Momentum is a real thing in a match, and to watch it swing only increases the intrigue. Every club and course should host regular matches across a variety of formats as a means for filling the tee sheet. It's time to promote match play as the preferred method for playing the game. A regular round of golf is leisure, but a match is a sporting pursuit. That way of thinking is worth courting to our American game again.

Courses need to be dog-friendly

It is hard to imagine a better pairing than dogs and golf. One of the greatest joys that I have found in the game is playing with my dog at my side. In Scotland, a dog is a welcome companion on the golf course. American golf courses would be wise to embrace our four-legged friends as part of the culture of the game. If golf is to become a great pastime in our country, then dogs must be allowed to walk at our side. Golf is the perfect opportunity to "take the dog for a walk," and courses could see added rounds by allowing such activities. Owners must keep their end of the bargain and make sure dogs are well behaved, but most courses have golfers that treat the grounds worse than a dog would. There aren't many games that allow pets to tag along, but golf is well suited for the canine. What a fun notion to think that both a dog and an owner can find equal enjoyment in a sport like golf. Dogs make for great playing partners and inviting them to the course is a great way to make any round more enjoyable.

Kids under 15 should play for free

Children should always be allowed to play golf for free. No matter the course or club, kids need to be openly encouraged to become golfers. The potential loss of small amounts of revenue has a marginal impact on the bottom line, but the gain of new golfers is desperately needed and can be undoubtedly lucrative for all. Kids that learn the game early in life stand a strong chance of staying in the game for decades to come. An added bonus is that children who get hooked on the game while playing free will likely insist on playing with their paying parents more. If we are going to talk about growing the game, then we must be serious about how we offer our courses to children. Like any budding relationship, the first impressions we make on children who are interested in golf will dictate how well they take to the game. I suggest the cutoff for free golf be after age 15, because I believe that teens should get a job at the course to earn free golf and learn more about how courses work. It's time to get serious about recruiting the next generation of golfers, and offering kids free rounds is a great place to start.

Golf style should adopt a more casual appearance

Golf needs to loosen up a bit if we want to attract new and younger players. There is nothing wrong with playing in a T-shirt, and not every top needs to be tucked in. Forgive my intrusion into traditional clubs and courses that have strict dress codes, but it is time that we allow a bit

66

more leeway in the attire of our game. The business world is continually changing what kinds of dress are allowed at the office, and the golf courses of America need to do the same. Instead of promoting certain types of clothing, why not promote the idea of being stylish? Stylish attire should be the mark we aim for as we broaden the game's appeal to millennials and members of Gen Z. Let's not tell people what they can or can't wear. A better path is to show people that golf is an opportunity to express your personal style while enjoying a great recreational and communal activity.

There should be new varieties of golf offered across the country

Golf can be played virtually everywhere. The game is played anytime there is a club, a ball, and a hole available. In today's world where time constraints are a constant, we must strive to provide opportunities for golf on smaller scales and in more convenient places. Golf should not be relegated to the open spaces on the edge of cities or on remote rural backroads. Why not create community putting courses in city parks or pitch-and-putts tucked into urban greenways? Playgrounds across the country offer basketball hoops and swing sets, so there could also be a space for a small chipping green. Office parks could have three to five one-shot holes available for people on their lunch break, and apartment buildings could offer a synthetic green on a pool deck or roof. If we want to bring more people to golf in the future, we may just have to bring more golf to where they are. Let's get creative and build small doses of golf all around us.

Golf in America has a promising future, but to arrive at the best possible outcomes, we must be willing to make a few needed course corrections. Golf needs to be promoted as a pastime and made open and affordable to the masses. The game should resemble the diverse tastes of new generations, and we must prioritize having fun through the sport in varied ways. If America's golf stakeholders are committed to growing the game, then we must be strategic in how we advance the best attributes of it. American golf has had many years of growth in its past, but in order to grow again, the game has to evolve in ways that better reflect the true spirit of the game.

12

Into the Mystic... Hangovers, Metaphysics, and the Round of My Life

T he hangover was a serious problem. I felt it as soon as the alarm
went off, and it hit me right between the eyes. Reaching for a glass
of water by my bed, I climbed out of another hazed awakening in the
rental condo that was ground zero for my golf vacation. Our annual guys
trip always makes for a few tough mornings, but that day was the worst
yet. We had a high noon tee time on the hardest course in America, and
my head felt like I had been kicked by a mule.

The Ocean Course at Kiawah Island Golf Resort has one hell of a
reputation. It hosted and roasted the best players in the world during
both the 1991 Ryder Cup and the 2012 PGA Championship. From the
tips, it boasts the highest course and slope rating combination in all of
America. Architect Pete Dye carved the course out of the South Carolina
coast, creating a Molotov cocktail of sand, water, and wind. From its
debut in the Ryder Cup matches to everyday resort guest play, the
Ocean Course has been dismantling golfers for nearly three decades.
Trust me when I say that trying to tackle such a place while battling the
demons of the night before is ill-advised.

The steady decline of my alcohol tolerance had been brought on
by my rapid acceleration into marriage, fatherhood, and life in my
early thirties. I am reminded of this each time I travel with our gang.

As I shuffled my way through a muddled morning routine, it became increasingly evident that I may be trading birdie putts for blowing chunks on the Ocean Course. It was a terrible feeling.

The first time I played the Ocean Course was on my honeymoon. It was a glorious day with my new bride and I loved the golf course, but my game was not up for the test. I'll never forget how much the wind blew my shots around while inflating my score that afternoon. I spent four years dreaming of a redemption round, and as that tee time finally approached, I was laid up on a couch watching the ceiling spin.

The heat index was creeping up on triple digits as we pulled up to the bag drop, and the stiff wind made it feel like we were under a hairdryer. I was headed for sweaty mess territory, but I had to press on. If I bailed on our group of fifteen guys, I'd never live down the shame. The only way through that black hole was straight on to the other side.

After consuming an antidote of Gatorade, Aleve, and CBD oils, I managed to make it to the driving range for a warm-up session. That's where I met Mike, my looper for the day. We made some small talk, and he chuckled as guys were giving me hell for my obvious struggles. The ball was flying all over the place, and the pounding headache made it hard to find any rhythm at all. The sun was straight above our heads, and I was sinking low as we boarded the transport to the first tee.

Nausea did seem to displace the nerves at least. I remembered the first hole well, and I asked Mike to hand me a hybrid to start the day. "I need to ease into this thing," I told him. With a deep breath and a slow turn, I sent the ball on its way. Through my squinting stare I watched the shot sail out in front of our group, and I found the first of many fairways that day. I grabbed another water and prayed that I could repeat that move a few more times. Luckily someone was listening.

The bogey-bogey start was less than impressive, but I felt like the ball was going where I wanted. On the third hole, I faced dire straits when my approach bounded over the buried boxcar green. I needed an up and down to get a par on the board, but my wedge game was feeling less than great. "Let me see that putter Mike." My caddie companion obliged, and from twenty feet off the green, I rolled the ball up to within a snuggly distance to the pin. It was just the spark I needed. Mike gave me a nudge of encouragement, and we pressed on.

Somehow, I was able to string together a series of par saves that included a wide variety of results. I putted from off the green a few more times to kick in range and even managed to clip the pin on an overcooked bunker shot. I knew that the scores were being authored by a shaky hand, but strangely they kept coming in at par. I was managing my game and my condition about as well as I could have hoped for. There was no way to know what would happen next.

The wind continued to intensify as we walked up to the ninth hole. It was blowing something fierce, and through the clouds of my mental state, I recognized the prevailing winds from my first time on the course. As my playing partners sized up their challenges, I stood on a hill facing the same shot I had four years prior. That's when I heard a faint voice whisper, "Ride the wind." I'm not sure if it was Bagger Vance, Shivas Irons, James Earl Jones, or God, but something told me what to do, and suddenly I was overcome with calmness. The peaceful feeling was unlike anything I've ever felt on a golf course.

I focused on the shot at hand and made a mighty swing of a six iron. The ball climbed high up against the gusting wind to form a towering draw. I could see the flight pattern illuminate before me, and the ball nestled to within ten feet of the cup. I missed the putt, but when we climbed into the shuttle for the tenth tee I became convinced that I had just unlocked some new form of my highest potential.

If you have ever found this feeling before you will know what I mean, but if not, you may think I'm nuts. My mind was entering into what felt like a trance. I had experienced this before, but it is rare and I never know how long it will last. On a day when my body was ready to give up on me, my mind found the extra gear I needed. Dare I say it, but I was in the zone.

The ensuing back nine was a bit of a blur. Facing thirty-plus mile per hour winds, I was sliding into some sort of hypnotic state. There was chaos all around me as my playing partners were losing their balls and their patience, but I barely saw them. Mike was there with me for yardages, but in hindsight, I don't remember a word he said along the way. While my friends were battling the course, I felt like I had found the cheat codes to a video game.

Then the putter got hot.

After a series of swings that set me up for scoring, I made birdie putts at 11 and 12 while nearly clipping a "turkey"—three in a row—at the 13th. The cup was starting to look like a basketball hoop, and on each stroke I saw my immediate future. I could visualize my arms raised, and a confident fist pump gesture following another holed putt. All I had to do was let it happen, and I did.

In those moments, my hands weren't my hands. In my mind, I was Seve Ballesteros. There was new and radiant energy emitting from my body as I glided from shot to shot. The feeling was euphoric.

At the 14th hole, we turned our backs to the wind and began the home stretch march to the clubhouse. I could sense that the round still had much to give. There was more joy yet to come, and it was predetermined to be my day. Despite a bogey, I rebounded by pouring in par putts at the 15th and 16th to keep the momentum alive. As I walked over the dune to the difficult 17th hole, I found myself wandering in and out of consciousness. The everyday noise that stifles my thoughts had gone silent, and at that moment I was one with the game.

From the tee box, I could see the ocean to my right. The waves were crashing up and down the beach, and the timing of it all acted like a metronome in my mind. Perched on the horizon was the stately clubhouse with a series of flags waving at a frantic pace. This would be the site of another special moment. I unleashed the smoothest of swings, and the ball carried dutifully toward the flag. It landed in the center green and careened off a slope towards the hole. I walked up to the green knowing I would make the putt.

In the pond between the dunes and the green, there was the largest alligator I've ever seen in my life. My confidence had reached such a level that I felt like I could ride him if I wanted to. Everything was in slow motion, and once again the people playing with me disappeared. The putt slid slightly down the hill and found the center of the cup. I stuck my putter in the air and turned my attention to the finale.

Mike the caddie pointed to the left side of the clubhouse and said, "Put her right there and let it ride." I just nodded at him with a quiet affirmation. Like many swings that day, I made a pass at the ball that resulted in something magical. The cut spin on the shot was shaping the ball flight perfectly into the fairway, and I looked back at my caddie as if the day would never end. Unfortunately there was an end, and as we walked up the 18th hole it was clearly in sight.

We walked at a steady but slowing pace up the fairway of the final hole. The crowded clubhouse veranda was now populated by the late afternoon onlookers who watch golfers come off the course each day. Draped in summer attire with cocktails in hand, they were the gallery who bore witness to the best round of my life. But like many stories, the ending was amiss.

When I arrived at my ball in the 18th fairway I looked up to take in the scene around me. For the first time in hours, I became cognizant of my friends. They were looking at me from forty yards away in the same manner that baseball teammates stay away from a pitcher with a perfect game on the line. Seeing them and the crowd of onlookers and the sea crashing nearby brought me back to where I was. I'll never know why, but as I took a long gaze at my surroundings, the cloud I was on seemed to lower back down to earth.

My approach to the final green came up well short, and I could feel myself returning to my body. I wasn't watching from above anymore. I was on the ground and in my shoes again. Perhaps it was because I realized a birdie would yield an even-par round, but either way, the golf gods had determined that my time was up.

Instead of a perfect finish, I tapped in for a bogey. It didn't matter though. I had just come through something that defied logic. It was supernatural. I had floated and glided and sailed gently around the hardest course in the country while battling a hangover and a two-club wind. Mike put on a big smile and congratulated me on a special round. My friends stood and stared at me like I had just performed some sort of miracle.

"Holy shit man."

"That was really something."

"I've never seen anything like that."

We exited the green and the round came to an end. The sun was beginning to lie down over the dunes, and happy hour was in full swing. I strolled up the gentle slope to the clubhouse veranda and finally paused to appreciate what I had just done. My score was 74. It wasn't the lowest of my life, but that round was by far the best I ever had. By this time, my hangover had subsided and our larger group was anxious to know how our foursome had fared. After all, there was money and pride on the line. I walked into the Ryder Cup bar and a smile climbed across my face. It was the happiest I'd ever been in golf.

What began as a dreadful morning had morphed into a day that I'll never forget. I don't know what happened out there on the Ocean Course, yet I'm confident that it was metaphysical in nature. People will call me crazy for suggesting that the game of golf left me with an out of body experience, but it happened and it was incredible. My round of golf that day was only possible because I allowed myself to go into something that I didn't fully understand. I've got a feeling that the hangover from those feelings won't be so easily shaken.

There is no way to know if I'll ever find that state of mind again. The golf gods are cruel and fickle. They tease us all with a poor sense of humor, but on occasion they breathe some powerful wind into our sails and carry us to newfound places. Such magic is real but fleeting. Just when we think we have harnessed its power, it disappears like a kite lost on the breeze. On my day at the Ocean Course, golf became a portal to another plane of existence. Perhaps, if I'm lucky and mix my spirits just right the night before, I can ride that wind again someday.

13

The People You Meet
When Playing

G olf is an introduction. If you let it, the game can facilitate
companionship in your life.

The first tee of a golf course is a fast track to making friends. Most
people who play golf are worth knowing, and discovering why is one of
the great joys of the sport.

The etiquette of golf, when properly exercised, is a road map for
relationship building. The stranger's hand you shake at the onset of a
round can become the familiar embrace of a friend only eighteen holes
later.

You and your playing partners will go through a lot together on the
golf course. You'll also go through a lot together in life. Because of those
similarities between the game and our existence, golf is a living network
of friends. Bonds are built over both bogeys and birdies. They are
cemented in the walks in between.

An outing with a new golf partner is an invitation to discovery.
Watch how they carry themselves, and listen to their personal story. An
interview through golf will reveal all you need to know about someone.

Let golf be your introduction to kindred spirits. The experiences you
have with someone today will eventually become the stories you tell as
old friends.

Golf is the great connector. The person you tee off with next might just change your life. The winning golfer is not judged by trophies—instead, they are measured by their friends. We succeed in this game by playing with those who share in our love for it. The people you meet when playing are the greatest reward golf can offer.

14

How I Learned to Play Faster Golf
...An Evening with Ran Morrissett

You can learn a lot about someone by playing golf with them. The ways in which a person conducts themselves on a golf course is a window into their character. Golf provides an ample display of one's disposition, and playing with others is an invitation to question our own comportment. Every so often, I have been graced with the chance to play golf with someone who challenges my assumptions and provides a model for how I might improve my own outlook on the game. Ran Morrissett is one such person.

Ran Morrissett is the founder and proprietor of Golf Club Atlas. CGA, as it is commonly called, is a website made for the study and discussion of golf course architecture. Instituted in the early days of the internet, GCA has become the go-to place for golfers to gain a deeper appreciation for the design of the best courses in the world. I have been a fan and message board member for a few years now, and Ran's writing and opinions on golf are among my favorite things to read. When the opportunity arose for me to travel to his home town near Pinehurst, North Carolina, I reached out to Ran to see if he may be available to talk some golf.

Ran is the kind of gentleman golfer with whom I find great delight in sharing a conversation. He is well traveled and fluent in the language of the game. These attributes became apparent upon my arrival at his home for our afternoon appointment. Ran was kind enough to take me up on having a chat, and he extended me a sincere and warm greeting. Ran suggested an itinerary for the evening that included a few holes of golf and some dinner. I was thrilled to join him for both, and it turned out to be quite the learning experience.

After a tour of his home and a brief walkthrough of GCA world headquarters, Ran and I loaded into his car and headed for his favorite golf hang — the Southern Pines Golf Club. On the ride over, he gave me some backstory on Southern Pines and its current state. The club has a rich history. Donald Ross designed its first nine holes in 1906 and eventually expanded the golf there to include 36 holes. Only 18 remain in play today. The club is owned by the local Elks Lodge which at one time made for steady traffic and a healthy level of revenues. Today, the club is dealing with the many effects of the ever-changing golf market.

When Ran and I pulled up to the club, I could immediately sense the aging of the place. In many ways, it reminded me of my home club. Time had moved on, but the club stayed behind. The large hulking and empty Elks Lodge casts a shadow on the first tee and serves as a monument to days gone by. Beyond the parking lot and the lodge, the property falls away into a pine forest that is populated with rolling hills. It is over those slopes that the routing of Donald Ross and the many charms of Southern Pines comes alive. It's the perfect place for Ran to have a hit in the fading sunlight of the sand hills each day.

After checking in, we were joined on the first tee by the delightful Chris Buie. Chris is one of the great resident writers and historians of the Pinehurst area. He also serves as Ran's regular playing partner at Southern Pines. Between the two of them, they figure to have logged a few thousand holes played under the evening sun there.

The preferred game for Ran and Chris is a fast-paced walk around the course. The score is largely irrelevant. Some nights they may only play a handful of holes, but most times they aim for around twelve. It is just enough golf to get some exercise and have a well-rounded conversation between the swings. For me to join them in this ritual was a great treat.

To say that Ran and Chris play briskly is an understatement. Even as a seasoned walker, I found myself having to adjust my pace to keep up. I would classify their methods as "reactionary" golf. The process of each shot was short and decisions were made quickly. Approach the ball, pull a club, swing, then start walking. It's that simple.

The way in which these gentlemen play is sporty and is in keeping with the traditions of the game in the United Kingdom. That can be attributed to the amount of time these gents have spent pursuing golf experiences around the globe. As Ran told me, "In other golfing nations, the pace just isn't an issue." Playing quickly is just common courtesy. "Nobody wants to see folks take two minutes over a three-foot putt. Just hit it and keep moving." During the course of our time together at Southern Pines, it occurred to me that this was a mindset worth emulating.

If I conjure an honest assessment of my game, I have to admit that my pace is often too slow. Perhaps it is due to the lingering effects of my junior golf career and all the crap I got fed about pre-shot routines and other manners of dragging on. Then again, it may just be that my inner demons won't allow me to carry as quickly as I should. Either way, my pace has been and remains something I must work on.

My conversion back into a walking golfer these past few years has helped a great deal. If you are the lone walker in a group, that reality necessitates you play fast enough to keep up. My pace has steadily improved, but it was my evening with Ran Morrissett that allowed me to see what I should be aiming for.

As we ventured around the course that evening, I became intoxicated by the rhythm that we were enjoying together. This was a pace in which many of the game's best aspects were made more readily enjoyable. For Ran and Chris, the golf being played was secondary to the pleasure of the walk with good company over a stunning layout.

There were times during my walk with Ran and Chris that I felt myself falling behind. Those guys really flew around the course. To tell the truth, it made me feel a bit inadequate. I can certainly see how newcomers to the game may feel completely lost at such a dizzying pace, but that was not an excuse that I had any room to enjoy. As a seasoned player, I needed to be better and as I watched my playing partners, I picked up on a number of customs that could easily be transferred to my own game.

The key to keeping up with Ran and Chris was to never stop moving. They showed me what is possible if you go to play with the intent of moving quickly around the course. For those of you wondering how this might play out in your own game, it means three things:

1. Be ready to hit as soon as it is your turn.
2. Once you start putting, don't stop until you hole out.
3. If you lose a ball, drop one and keep playing quickly.

Thanks to Ran and Chris, I found a strategy to improve my pace of play while having more fun on the course. The pace of play in golf continues to be a hot topic in the game, and with today's ever-growing social media conversations, there seems to be real momentum for speeding play across the globe. That is a good thing. For many years, I shrugged when my friends commented about my pace because I didn't believe them. "Surely it isn't me," I thought. But guess what — it was. Like anything else in life, I had to want to change if I ever hoped to improve.

By the time I arranged my meetup with Ran and round of golf with him and Chris, I was already on the path to improvement. They helped further my education, and ever since I have made serious headway in reducing my round times. With a hard-working wife and rambunctious toddler at home, I need to gain back all the time I can. It's still a work in progress, but I like where things are headed.

When Ran, Chris, and I finished our round at Southern Pines we scurried over to a local pub for some beers and a meal. For a guy like me, I could sit there and listen to their tales of golf trips all night. However, much like the way they play golf, dinner was straight to the point. We enjoyed every second together, but we all had other things to get to. That's the kind of golf I try to play more of these days—fun, faster, freewheeling, and far from caring too much about the score.

I'm not sure we will ever see that kind of pace catch on across the entirety of the American golf landscape, but it is an idea worth spreading. The concept of playing quickly is something golf and the folks who play it all need to embrace. I'm still working on it, but it feels good to play faster. For those who may need a lesson in picking up the pace, I suggest stopping into Southern Pines some evening and see if you can keep up with Ran and Chris.

15

Can You Dig It?
Going down the social media rabbit hole to find golf's newest venues for enjoying the game

M̲y truck was speeding around the curving streets of my neighborhood as I was rushing to get home before my wife. She didn't need to know what I was up to, and I didn't really know how to tell her. I was about to take a leap into the deep end of a pool that is the world of golf on social media.

I got through the door to our red brick home and immediately opened my computer. I pulled out my well-worn credit card and was fearful that she might walk in at any moment. I was startled when my phone vibrated; it was a text to signal that the link was live. I punched in my card numbers and purchased my ticket to the edge of the golfing world. "Pay now and don't get caught," I thought. I would have to explain to her later.

I was headed for a remote place in a distant state for a golf trip with strangers. I bought a spot for myself in a low-key meet-up of like-minded golf enthusiasts. The event was called The Shindig. It was forty guys with a mutual obsession for good golf and fellowship gathered at a nine-hole course in Tennessee. The Shindig was a rendezvous on the frontier of golf's new age, and it all came together because of Instagram.

Those of us who committed to attend were friends according to social media, but few had ever met in person. We knew of each other and understood each other in the sense that we all shared some common beliefs: Golf is meant for walking, course architecture matters, and stories of places that embrace these ideas should be shared with the masses.

This may sound like a cult preparing to drink the Kool-Aid that guarantees passage on the mothership, but it was really another sign of the arrival of golf's future. We were part of a different kind of golf club, non-exclusive in nature yet grounded in a common ideal: play or perish.

A few months after my clandestine credit card purchase was made in the shadows of my marriage, I found myself standing in a gravel parking lot in South Pittsburg, Tennessee. We were all there together at Sweetens Cove Golf Club trying to decipher which faces went with which of our favorite Instagram accounts. Some handshakes were exchanged and nervous laughter was heard as we stood around like kids at a middle school dance looking across the lot at each other. After many months of anticipation, we were standing there at last and only golf could break the ice.

Sweetens Cove is a monument to the belief that golf can be simple and fun at the same time as being challenging and interesting. It's a nine-hole course with no clubhouse or amenities, just pure golf. Sweetens represents the kind of golf that folks like me dream about while at work, or at the dinner table with kids, or scrolling through favorite golf accounts on social media during a wedding. The course has wide fairways, rolling contours, bold greens, and a requirement of strategic thinking and shot execution on every hole. Sweetens is one of the most interesting golf experiences in America, and by any measure, it is far outside of ordinary.

The Shindig was a gathering of golf vagabonds, some of golf's emerging social media influencers, and many men like myself who had a hard time explaining the trip to their wives. A description of what we were doing there was hard to come by. The organizers kind of like it that way.

The Shindig was the brainchild of Sugarloaf Social Club. Sugarloaf is a self-described group of like-minded golfers dedicated to the classical preservation, enjoyment, and creation of the game. The gents behind that vision, Ian Gilley and Harrison Lewis, were our guides and Sweetens Cove was our host.

Sugarloaf and Sweetens have something in common. Each of those entities are brands that have developed a national following almost entirely by the high-speed word of mouth that happens on social media today. Instagram, in particular, has introduced folks like the Sugarloaf guys to a weird new way of being famous.

Instagram users can seek out their preferred interests with laser-like focus. This has been particularly fruitful for golfers, especially the kind of us at The Shindig. We all were able to find each other because of Instagram. For many golfers, Instagram has become a way to discover new places with a particular appeal. To those of us standing in the gravel, Sweetens Cove was one of those places, and the Sugarloaf gang were the digital tour guides that helped us find it.

We began our rounds that morning as the last remnants of spring were dashing away. The humidity of a Southern summer was beginning to settle in for a four-month stay, and after a long winter, the course was turning greener by the day. The shotgun start was initiated soon after every player was awarded an armful of gifts. Head-covers, ball marks, leather goods, and braided belts were all included in the price of admission. Players gathered their Sugarloaf branded bounty and sprang for their respective starting holes.

For the next four hours, our band of misfit golfers marched through the mix of waste areas, expansive fairways, and contoured greens that occupy the terrain of that Tennessee mountain valley. These golfers moved across those grounds like a heard of elephants crisscrossing the African savannah. Swing, walk, and repeat. That was our formula for the day.

There were hoots and hollers heard from across the course all morning long. Beer coolers were strategically placed for bottomless brews to be a convenient grab-and-go along the way, and the smell of smoked pork was wafting over our heads. The golf at Sweetens Cove is as enjoyable as the mountains around the course are tall, and we were experiencing a version of it that most players will never know.

When the morning rounds were completed, it was time for a fresh plate of Tennessee barbecue. The plates were piled high with pork and chicken, and those meats were smothered in homemade slaw and sauces. The gravel lot got awfully quiet while we scarfed down the reward for our morning walk, but the laughter accelerated shortly after when the "shootout" began.

To determine a champion for our outing, the boys from Sugarloaf concocted a challenge that felt like a human Rube Goldberg machine. Players earning a spot in the shootout began by pouring a fresh beer into a large glass mug and from there were required to run down the hill to the extravagant ninth green. Players had to putt across the green and hole out before running back up the hill to our barbecue feast all while not spilling their beer. Points were awarded for most beer left, least strokes to hole the putt, and amount of time to finish. Only the worthiest would win the grand prize of a Sugarloaf custom Mackenzie golf bag.

After a champion was crowned, players began to tee off again for as much golf as possible. Clouds were gathering and thunder was rolling across the horizon as we began to play again. I had my persimmon woods in the bag this go around, and even the ominous afternoon forecast couldn't dampen my spirits. I was with my new friends, people who believe in golf like I do, and we were soaking up a most joyous occasion.

Somewhere on the second hole, the lightning reached our mountain valley and the golf would have to end. There was a rat-race for everyone to reach the parking lot as players jockeyed for a place in the shed. The shed is a 10x15 substitute for a clubhouse and is the only cover from the elements at Sweetens Cove. It was muggy and we were wet, but the beer was cold and the conversation was now forcibly close.

By this point in the affair, there were twenty or so players hanging on to hope and crammed into the close quarters of the Sweetens Cove shed. We were still committed to the small chance that the storm would pass and the golf would resume, but as the rain persisted players prepared to depart. One by one, those clinging to the dream of more blue sky and a few more holes peeled off to the parking lot and headed for home.

As things were getting a bit claustrophobic in the shed, I decided it was time to make a move to my truck and hit the road for the first leg of my journey home. I shook hands with many new friends on my way through the crowded shed. The rustle of rain gear was deafening in the small space, but I managed to exchange a few phone numbers on the way out. I wanted to be sure to stay connected to as many of these lads as I could. After saying my final goodbyes and see-you-laters, I made a sprint back across the gravel through the pounding rain and loaded up the truck for the long ride I had ahead.

Sitting in my truck, I could see the remnants of this great day through the swing of my windshield wipers. The parking lot was now half full and the porch of the shed was a little less crowded. The sunshine had been submerged in a dense downpour of rain. I wanted badly to get back out onto the course, but the time had arrived for me to turn the key, crank the truck, and leave.

The Shindig was everything I had hoped it would be. It lived up to the exciting expectations I had running through my head as I sped through the neighborhood racing to get home and secure my spot in the event. I was so happy to get to Sweetens Cove, and I was delighted by the prospects of the burgeoning friendships I had discovered there.

I am amazed that a photo sharing application on my phone has allowed me and many others like me to build and grow new networks of friends who have the same interests as I do. Wherever I travel to, I know I can find golfers of a common mind to mine that are always ready to play somewhere interesting. The barriers to connecting with adventurous and outgoing friends to play golf with are gone forever.

The Shindig was proof that golf still thrives where the experience is good and the people are passionate. Golf needs more experiences like the one that I had with my friends at Sweetens Cove. I'm talking about experiences that are made for the golfers that are consumed with the game.

Over the course of our time together at The Shindig, every player was posting photos, sharing stories, and most importantly inspiring followers to seek out the best kind of experiences that golf can offer. Golf will grow when the people who love it most can convince the undecideds that there is more to discover if you just take the next step down the rabbit hole.

The game will reach its fullest potential when there are more advocates for it like Sugarloaf Social Club. Golf needs advocates who not only tell stories, but organize events and bring people to the game. Golf is growing, and it will grow more when places like Sweetens Cove migrate from being an outlier to becoming the mainstream. Thanks to the internet and social media, the future of golf is arriving fast and there has never been a better time for the game to grow.

We now have entered the age of the golf-crazed vagabond, the emerging social media influencer, and the guys who have a hard time explaining to their wives why they are on the road again with their golf clubs. I'm excited to see where the game goes in the coming years, and I can't wait for the next adventure with my new friends. When I went to The Shindig, I jumped head first into golf's new world, and I can't wait to recruit more friends to take the plunge.

16

Golf Is Everywhere

Sometimes when I daydream
I lose myself in thoughts
About how everyday places
Could easily become golf holes.

The park out my office window
with the naturally sloping terrain
Is the perfect place for pitch shots
Beneath the skyline of the city.

There's a field of golden farmland
I pass while driving at dusk
To my parents' house for dinner
That should be a short par four.

When I walk down the beach
With my daughter in the sand
I ponder putting by the sea as
She climbs dunes on the shore.

When I stroll through the woods
During the cold months of winter

The tree-lined paths I hike on
Look like fairways in my mind.

The hillside by the highway
Where the old fence line stands
Has windblown bunkers guarding
A ridge that could be a green.

There is the quiet cove at the lake
Near the house I frequently visit
With a crested knoll on an isthmus
That is a par three shaped by God.

Beyond the asphalt runway
Of the airport I often fly from
There are gentle hills that roll
Over land clearly made for golf.

The steeples of the churches
In my old and quaint hometown
Would make a perfect aim point
For a par five down Main Street.

Then there's the winding stream
Which flows where I used to fish
While wondering what kind of shot
It would take to clear the bend.

On my way home from work
In a well-lit square downtown
Sits a perfect patch of grass
Where I could probably play at night.

I even make holes at my house
When I mow the lawn on Mondays
Following around the flower beds
Which my wife keeps finely pruned.

The places I imagine playing
Are merely figments in my mind
Which I conjure up for pleasure
Because for golf, I have no time.

Life won't lend me the freedom
To spend my days out on the course
So I see holes all around me
Which may very well be worse.

Perhaps I'm just plain crazy
And the game has made me so
But I find some comfort knowing
That golf is everywhere I go.

17

How to Travel for Golf:
Thoughts on where to go, how to be there, and what to remember

To be a golfer is to be a wanderer, and that is my identity. The game is, at its very essence, a walkabout through the fields, forests, towns, and dunes of the world. For that reason, a golfer's soul yearns to journey. As a golfer, my thirst for adventure is unquenchable.

For those like me who are inflicted with such a love for the game, one foot will always be compelled to follow the other. Each round of golf creates a longing for the next. In my mind, there lies an uncontrollable urge to stray and a sense that each new course needs to be further from home than the last.

The golfer is a traveler and an explorer. No destination will ever satisfy the desire to see another. I am a golfer, and I am increasingly compelled to roam.

The passages of golf books become the places that yield sunburns on my skin. Reading about distant lands isn't enough to cure my curiosity though. I have to see it with my own eyes and play the course with clubs in tow.

There is a brilliant sun shining on the fairways in my mind, and if I can muster up a willingness to set forth, I can find that warmth in living color. When presented with the opportunity to travel for golf, I exhaust every means to make it happen.

That being said, to reach an awareness of the available adventures in the sport is to suffer madness. This comes from the knowledge that I'll never be able to experience them all.

Which brings me to the following passages.

No golf traveler is alike, yet there is a kinsmanship found among those of us who spend hours searching out the next stop on the journey. Opinions on courses, clubs, and destinations for golf will vary, making it important to remember that the objective of traveling is to form your own. Every course in the world has something to offer the golfer on the move, but how can one best discern what to seek out next?

For that question, I offer you these thoughts.

Where to go...

Go in search of great walks.

Not every golf course can be walked, but those most worthy of your time will be of the variety you explore on foot. The game was meant for walking, and the best golf in the world will always be that which is tailored to such methods of play. When traveling, the walks should actually be the reason for the trip. Golf is just an excuse to go for the hike. Take these considerations in mind when evaluating where you'd like to walk next.

Seek out an understanding of architecture.

Architecture is the field in which art and science meet. The designing of golf courses is consistent with that truth. Golf course architects are both artist and engineer. No two sites for golf are the same, and every architect has a different lens on the world; therefore each individual course is a separate and unique expression of those who built it. The seasoned golf traveler is keen to this, and through earned knowledge of the subject, one can find a greater appreciation for all aspects of the game. The study of a course's design should be a leading factor in choosing where to play.

Account for the history of a place.

History provides the context for how a place came to be. Strive to be a traveler who wonders why things are a certain way, and you'll find history has the answers. When traveling to a new golf course, a review of its history should always be the appetizer before the main course of playing there. Golf has long been a game with a reverence for its roots and an appreciation of its past. Many clubs and courses offer visitors the chance to learn their story, and others can be found through simple research. To not seek such details is to willingly avoid the full experience. Not every great course has a long history, but those that do often offer a more interesting destination.

Consider the available accommodations.

The place in which you lay your head should never be an afterthought. Some locations offer luxurious quarters while others are more spartan, but I would suggest proximity to places of interest as a more pressing need. Look for lodging that serves as a window into the community or perhaps a room located on-site that may yield additional time spent at the course. The hotel by the highway may suffice for bedding and such, but a better experience can be found at the course cabin, bed-and-breakfast, or charming hotel downtown. Where you stay will dictate where you eat, where you drink, and where you roam while visiting a place for golf. With that in mind, be sure to choose wisely and aim for places that increase the odds of serendipitous discoveries and a better understanding of the destination.

Making a decision on where to go is only the first step. There is also the matter of being in a place. How does one compose oneself when traveling for golf, and what should you be looking for?

These are my recommendations.

How to be there...

Observe the presentation of the golf course.

Golf courses are works of art constructed on a medium of grass. With a live and growing canvas, the state of a golf course is always in flux. Knowing this, the golf traveler should make sure to appreciate the state of the course. The superintendent, whose role it is to oversee the presentation of the playing surface, is oftentimes the unsung hero of the golf world. The agronomists that maintain the turf are essential to every pleasant golf experience, and the traveler should take note of the conditions that were carefully arranged for them. Be sure to thank the agronomy staff should your paths cross while playing.

Speak with those who work there.

To best understand a place, one must speak with those who tend to it. The staff members of any golf facility are the keepers of valuable information and important details. Some professionals will offer delightful details about a golf course unsolicited, but others may require the spark of conversation. Engaging with staff is a wonderful way to make a new acquaintance while also seeking out the best ways to enhance your visit. Present yourself and your questions with a genuine curiosity, and oftentimes you will be rewarded with local tips, unique stories, or perhaps even a tour. These are the interactions that often lead to repeat visits and intimate discoveries during your stay. Travelers need not be shy; the staff is there to answer your questions and ensure you have a great day at the course.

Cater to the customs of the regulars.

When visiting a club or course, it is best to try and enjoy the facilities in the same manner as the regulars do. Whether you are an invited guest or simply paired with strangers, be sure to yield to the resident customs. There may be a particular game you will be asked to join or perhaps the norm is to play from a closer tee box than you are accustomed, either way — go with the flow. Those who play there the most likely know how to play it for maximum enjoyment, and as a traveler that should be your aim as well. You never know, by following the regulars you might just find something worth changing in your own golf routine.

Look for where the locals go.

When traveling for golf, the time spent on the course is only part of the trip. There should be dining, shopping, sightseeing, and other exploratory activities on the itinerary. Some research before your travel is critical, but more importantly, ask the locals where they like to go. More times than not the best places in town will be those which the residents frequent. This also holds true for golf. Be sure to save some time in your travels for the course you didn't expect to play. A local recommendation can make for a splendid emergency nine holes or a quick round before heading home. Ask around for advice on all counts of your trip and allow for pleasant surprises.

The trip doesn't end on the final green or even when you put the clubs back in your garage. Some trips never really end at all. The best travels are the kind that are permanently extended in our memories. The trips that change how we see things become chapters in our ever-evolving story.

Here are my recommendations on how to maximize the impacts of your travel.

What to remember...

Document your days spent away from home.

There has never been an easier time in history to chronicle your observations from traveling. Technology allows us to record the details of our trips via a wide variety of social media, applications, and other means. Of course, there is always the more traditional route of handwritten journal entries or even blogging. No matter your preferred method, be sure to take some time each day of your trip and make a few notes on what you have seen. There is great joy to be found in recounting your travels while reading the details of days gone past.

Take time to reflect on your experiences.

In many ways, golf is a meditation. Arranging your thoughts from a golf trip is a healthy way to find some peaceful appreciation for what you have seen. Beyond the time you spend on the golf course, it is important to set aside some moments for the quiet contemplation of your experience. It is in those minutes, spent reflecting on your trip, in which clarity can emerge in your thinking. Oftentimes, I have found that my most meaningful takeaways from golf travel occur long after the initial experience has happened. Through a deliberate search of my thoughts, I find new ways of seeing the places that I visited months or years before.

Tell your friends about where you went.

Sharing the stories of your golf travels is an important part of being an explorer in our game. Please note that this is not an invitation to display braggadocios behavior. Your aim should be to provide valuable insights into the places you have been. Be a guide to those who may want to set forth on their own discovery someday. Do not instruct them, but instead, offer some seeds from which they can grow their own ideas and opinions. Discussing a trip with those you shared it with or others who saw the same place on another occasion is one of the great joys of golf.

Contemplate how the trip has changed your perspective.

The best travels are the ones that change how you see the world. For golfers, that can occur in a wide variety of ways. Perhaps a course has shifted your thoughts on a particular architect, or maybe a previously undiscovered golf culture made you swoon for a new city. The possibilities are as endless as your list of courses yet to be seen. The notes you write, the conversations you have, and the memories you make while traveling for golf all add up to shape your unique perspective on the game. When you think you have finally landed on a set of beliefs about golf, then it's time to hit the road again. The next course may just be the one that changes your mind forever. The only way to know is to go, and once you've been, only you can determine what it all meant.

Traveling for golf is a means for replenishing my soul. The game has always had a hold on me, and with each trip I take I find new inspiration for living life as a golf enthusiast. Some places speak to me more than others, but with each new stop along the way, I find small traces of the game's deeper meaning. For me, traveling for golf is a transcendent pursuit.

So, my charge to you, my fellow golf traveler, is this: Go forth and seek out the courses that call your name. Find the time to venture for golf and be sure to savor each step. Seek out stories, architects, history, and new scenery. Search for the places that will shape you for the better, and never stop discovering what the game can mean in your life. There are many people who share your passion for golf, and the best way to find them is to start looking wherever you may roam. Golf is a grand adventure, but it's up to us to take it.

I hope to see you out there on fairways near and far.

18

A Simple Game
for Troubled Times

L ife is hard, and so is golf. I suppose that makes it odd that I use one
to escape the other. When things get overwhelming, I always look
for my clubs and a good long walk to save me from myself and the world
around me. I run to the golf course in an effort to create separation
between me and whatever might be troubling my mind. I have found
peace through playing alone, but it is when I play with others that I
discover just how wonderful people are to be around. It is in those
moments when the problems of our lives are put on the shelf that I find
great joy in being with my fellow man. Golf is a game meant to bring
people together, and God knows we need more of that these days.

The world we know today is filled with difficulty and unrest. Things
don't quite seem right, and I think we all feel that some change is needed.
The news stories we find on our timelines and TV screens seem to get
worse each week. Shootings at home, tensions abroad, and a never-
ending stream of disagreement among political factions are all symptoms
of the same problem. We have misplaced our ability to treat each other
with respect and dignity. In these troubling times, we need to forge new
ways for people to find one another and enjoy our common traits. For this
reason, I believe we could all use a little more golf in our lives.

Despite the occasional grim realities of our time, hope has not been lost. The good people still outnumber the bad, and if history tells us anything, we will someday find solutions to sort all this madness out. That doesn't mean it will be easy, but in order to make a course correction, we have to learn to be around each other again. In my experience, that is exactly what golf offers the world.

Golf is a means for spending time with your friends, family, colleagues, and neighbors. Our game has always been intended as a pastime, and today we need social agreements like this in the worst of ways. I have known many truths about golf over the years, and the greatest of these is that because the game strips us of our differences, it opens a window to create new and lasting relationships.

Golf offers those who play it the chance to see others as fellow travelers on the same journey. Golf reminds us of our shared struggle and connects us through a camaraderie which only our agonizing game can create. On the golf course, we all have much more in common than our backgrounds and beliefs would allow us to appreciate. To put it simply, we are all just trying to move the ball down the fairways of life, and golf serves as a way to see that truth.

Recently, when greeted with another morning of disturbing headlines, I picked up the phone and called my parents. In that call, I invited my dad to come over and play golf with me. We made some plans for a quick nine holes and dinner afterward at the house. Perhaps it was because the horrifying stories of another mass shooting got me thinking about my family, or maybe I just wanted to see my folks, but either way, I set up some time for golf and I sure am glad I did.

Dad and I have had our differences over the years. Sometimes they have been over politics, and on other occasions, it may have just been family issues. Our relationship is great these days, and golf is a meaningful way to spend time with him. When he and Mom got to my house, I took him up to the course for a brisk evening walk before dinner. With my dog at our side, we walked nine holes under a brilliant summer sunset.

During our round, we spoke about the joy my daughter has brought us both, my budding career, his pending retirement, and other matters of interest to the two of us. No debates, no bother, just a father and son connecting on the course. The walk was splendid, and our dinner afterward was delightful. Having my family sit down at the dinner table and enjoy a meal and conversation was exactly what I needed after a weekend filled with bad national news. As my parents left for the night, I couldn't help but think how wonderful the time together had been. It made me consider how fortunate we all are to have each other. I was also reminded of how much the world could use the kind of fellowship Dad and I shared on the course that night.

Spending time playing with Dad and enjoying a nice dinner with my family left me with a peaceful feeling. When I woke up the next morning to start my week, I felt a renewed hope for a better world. Imagine what more of that feeling could do for us all.

Having golf in my life has granted me an improved mental state and more stable relationships. Through the years, golf has taught me how to build new friendships and rekindle old ones. The game has shown me how to overcome my prejudices and led me to build upon my best qualities. Golf has saved my life on more than one occasion, and it has unquestionably made me a better man.

I don't have all the solutions to the world's problems, but I do know this: If we can all commit to spending time with one another in search of our better angels, then things will certainly improve. To do that, we need systems that allow for a certain kind of nearness with the ones we love, folks we know, and even those we disagree with. Golf is one of those systems.

I want to play more golf because the game makes me feel better about myself and the world around me. It's therapeutic, and it activates the best of my thoughts. I believe that to be true of others who play as well. Beyond self-improvement, golf gives us enough time together to see how much we have in common. If I can make a commitment to playing more golf with my family, friends, colleagues, and neighbors then perhaps I can have a small impact on the world.

Our times may be troubled, but we have to avoid the convenience of isolation. We must choose to lean in and engage with one another. I propose that we spend less time in the bowels of the internet and more time crossing paths on the fairways and greens of the local golf course. Golf can be a mechanism for change, and it starts with those of us who play the game deciding to bring more people into it.

The world may be in peril, and the situations of our daily existence often seem dire, but there are still means for bridging our divides. My preferred method involves a small white ball and club with which to hit it. The pursuit of this game has always been a path to my best self, and if a lost soul like me can find a way to improve so might others. So, the next time you read a bad headline or experience a tense moment in your day, think of someone you know who may be in need of nine holes and a walk with a friend. Go play golf and remember all the things right with the world and with the people in it. The game we love is a simple one, yet its impacts on those who play it can be profound. Golf can't solve all our problems, but it is certainly a good place to start.

About the Author

Jay Revell is a golf writer based in
Tallahassee, Florida. His stories, essays,
travelogues, and histories have been
featured in a wide variety of popular
publications including *The Golfer's
Journal, McKellar Magazine*, Golf.com, and
Golf Advisor. Jay has also worked with a
number of golf-relevant brands such as
MacKenzie Golf Bags and Visit Florida.
He publishes regular musings on the
game via his personal website JayRevell.com.

Beyond golf, Jay works as public affairs professional where he applies
over a decade of experience in the realms of public policy, advocacy,
public relations, and content creation for community-based causes,
campaigns, and other critical organizations at the local level.

Jay is a husband and father to his wife Sarah and daughter Winnie. He
lives with his family and their two wonderful dogs, Leon and Bodie. His
family, including their dogs, are featured prominently in his daily golf
stories published on his Instagram page.

Jay Revell can be reached in the following ways.

Email: jayrevelltlh@gmail.com

Twitter: @JayRevell

Instagram: @jayrevellwrites

Website: www.jayrevell.com

Made in the USA
Columbia, SC
11 May 2021